Writing & Ghost Writing

Tips, Hints, Tricks and Stories

Front Cover thanks to Pixabay from Pexels

Chapters

Chapter 1 So you want to be a writer?

If you are reading this, I think we can assume you would like to be writer and want to know more about it. The only other alternative is that you have come to the wrong place and it takes a while for this to sink into your brain. Either way you might as well read on, you might like what you see, you might learn something and at worst you can have a laugh.

Perhaps I am not the best person to advise on becoming a "good writer", but as I am a writer with a moderate level of success, (under another name), I hope to be able to give you some help.

Practice is very important as are correct spelling and grammer, and if this sentence made sense to you – you have a problem.

Practice is a noun, practise is a verb and is the correct one in this case. Grammar is not spelt "er" and a comma is missing from "important, as". Whether the "are" should be "is" or not, is a matter still being discussed by so-called professionals, but technically "is" is correct. This works on the 1 table and 4 chair basis; ie. "There are 4 chairs and 1 table", but "There is 1 table and 4 chairs", as the verb should agree with the first item in the list.

"Practice is very important, as is correct spelling and grammar."

Lesson over, but hopefully the point was made, (and the first version will pass most grammar checkers with only "grammar" changed). There is little point in writing if you still need to learn the language, so learn it first, then write. That done, try to find a subject that interests you, but that will also interest other people. If it interests you, you will be able to write better, in more flowing sentences and with feeling, but, if you want people to read it, it is not enough to be well written, it needs to interest the reader.

Now that you have a finished article, story or book – that you have read at least once, if not twice, to check for spelling, punctuation and any other errors, what to do with it becomes the next problem.

A good idea at the beginning of your, no doubt, illustrious career, is to find a place to publish an article or short story so that the public can give you feedback on both subject matter and writing skills. There are many you can try, and really one is much like another. Each has pros and cons, so read the guidelines and any feedback from writers already using the site and choose the one most suited to your needs.

Do not take criticism too seriously on these sites. A number of frustrated people just go there to be nasty, but what will give you an idea of the value of your work, are the positive comments – do people like it, did it leave them with questions, (that means something was not explained well), did it get many hits, and so on.
You can always start with free sites that accept most any work and if your work was well received there, start looking for paying jobs writing articles or stories, and good luck.

Chapter 2 Can You Earn Money Writing?

You want to be a writer, now that begs the question – Can you earn a living writing? Well the answer is yes, you can.

However, and this is the critical point, probably not in the way you imagined. Do not despair or give up, there are ways round this – if you are lucky. It is only a question of being prepared to face what you need to do, to get where you want. This part is not designed to put you off, but rather prepare you for the difficulties and offer alternatives while you are waiting to be discovered.

Dreams of being a writer usually involve writing a best seller.

Well, forget it! Unless you have a backup fund the size of Bill Gate's, or are one of the luckiest people in the world, forget it – for now.

Only a few lucky ones actually make it as a bestselling writer, we all know that. What maybe you don't know, is this;

The majority of publishers, and even agents, do not accept unsolicited manuscripts. That means they only accept work they asked for. This is back to the classic 'you can't get work without experience, but you can't get experience because no one will give you work,' that applies to any job.

Leaving that aside and assuming you find a publisher to accept your work and they read it, here is what can happen next.

Let's assume you are a brilliant writer and destined to have success, (so about 0.001% of the writing community). You write a best seller and send it to publishers, magazines and so on. Now, an average time for any type of reply is around six to eight months I have had a few replies after a month and others more than two years later. All that time you had no income.

Now, let's assume, again, they like it and send a contract, which you don't sign without expert advice. This costs money and takes time. It can take another six months, and believe me you need to check the contract carefully. I have had clauses such as, "Anything written belongs to them and they get a percentage – a large percentage".

Now I write the odd quiz and logic problem, because I enjoy it and it gives me a bit extra spending money. I also do some translations for a reasonable amount, but that contract meant the publisher got their share, (40%), of any of this work too. That made doing other work virtually pointless, as I was left with too small an amount, so I had to ask to change the contract. About three months and many messages later I got an answer. They wouldn't change it, so that didn't work out and I had to start again to try and find another publisher, having lost about nine months or a year waiting time.

The next contract I was offered said, "I confirm the work is all my own and does not infringe on anyone's rights in any way," that was fine as it was a total work of fiction. However, the contract continued, "And I accept responsibility if anyone files a claim against the published book for any reason." Earlier in the contract it had said, "The publisher has the right to edit in any way they see fit and to publish and distribute however they wish." When you put these two parts together you get – the publisher can change the names and places to real people and places, but if the real people sue, it is my responsibility.

In this instance I tried again to get the contract modified to say, "I accept responsibility for what I wrote, as I wrote it, and only that". After months of deliberation and messages they agreed.

I would say this probably reflects my fortunes with my work, win one, lose one, but that gives me an average time of at least two years between having work accepted, and a lot of time without any earnings.

I was also offered a couple of contracts where the publisher put up half the money and I was to fund the rest. I refused. Here is why; I would have bene paying a few thousand to get my book published when I can do that through Amazon or Lulu for free. The publisher said they would publicise my work, but if they didn't believe in it enough to pay all the expenses, (a drop in the ocean for them), how well will they push sales? Also, they all publish books in the traditional way where they put up all the money for the book, so they are more likely, if not certain, to push the book that cost them money rather than mine, which they have already been paid for. It just seems like a half way measure, but half way to nowhere, and not something worth paying for. If you publish your book yourself, for free, think how much advertising you can do if you spend the £3,000+ on that, rather than give it to a publisher who feels it isn't worth their effort to spend money on.

Unless you are lucky enough to be J.K. Rowling and make a few million from one book, (unfortunately I haven't got close to that sort of money for my books, even though they are just as good, naturally – tongue in cheek, you have large periods with no income.

If you have a trust fund, a rich husband or some other means which provides enough money to live on, great. Otherwise you need to make the money for bills and food yourself, and as a writer there are three basic ways that work for me.

One is to join writing sites, and there are four that work for me. 'Chapter 2 Where to Earn Money Writing Until your Book Takes Off'. I have listed them and explained how they work, the pros and cons and what to look out for.

Another is to be a ghost writer, and in the chapter, "All You Need to Know About being a Ghost Writer", I have set out some tips and offered advice based on my own experiences.

Lastly is writing for magazines, businesses and private clients without working through sites, and again I have shared my experience in the chapter "Writing for Private Clients".

Chapter 3 Writing Tools; Both Useful ones and others which are a Terrible Hindrance

At times writing is not the biggest problem for a writer, it is all the surrounding bits and pieces that can be as much, if not more, of a headache. This may be ideas about where to find good free images to add value to a piece of work, synonyms to use in place of another word that perhaps is already included in the article and many other things. This section aims at helping writers with these dilemmas by suggesting free sites for many of these added difficulties.

Grammar Checkers are Usually Wrong

Writers Bane, Automatic Grammar Checkers

It appears to be a recognised fact among English scholars, that grammar checkers do not work, yet an increasing number of people are starting to believe them a substitute for human checking.

There is no doubt they are quicker, and save time – but what is the point of saving time if the answer is wrong. Anyone could do the sum; 132,458,794 multiplied by 67.376, divided by 58999 in three seconds if you did not want the correct answer, (151266.02). You simply hit the first number buttons you come across, and the sum is done.

This applies to all grammar checkers, but the one I tested the most is the one on everyone's lips, Grammerly.

Grammar checkers miss important errors, suggest corrections that are inaccurate and flag grammatically correct text as incorrect – to say nothing of marking "other" English as wrong. An American checker marks British English as wrong and vice versa, never mind Australian, Irish or Canadian English.

One of the problems is that "word usage" can directly influence the tone of a sentence, but computers do not understand "tone". There are also many ways to say the same thing and many expressions that have numerous meanings, and here again a computer does not recognize these inflections or differences.

Putting this simple text - up to this point - through what is supposedly one of the best grammar checkers gave this result; This article is incorrect and results only 51% correct. Improvements need to be made to bring it up to standard.

This is the analysis;

The original word in British English "recognised" had to become "recognized" to pass, and be considered correct, even though I entered British English as my language.

Mechanical grammar checkers appear to have a problem distinguishing "between, (for two items), and among, (for more than two)", so in this article "between English scholars" is marked as correct "as there are not more than two items spoken about in the article", (this is what it told me), and among is incorrect and lowers my score, even though 'between' is not correct and 'among' is.

Abbreviations are wrong, in any circumstances, and there are no exceptions, the checker said. "An American" is wrong because the program says to "Use "a" before words that start with consonants", so the article before American needs changed. Why the program thinks American starts with a consonant is anybody's guess.

"One of the problems" is considered too 'wordy', and in order to pass, needs to be "one problem", (even though this is not the same thing.). The sentence with "effect the tone" had to be changed from "affect the tone", – yet interestingly when it was changed, the program said, it was wrong and it then needed changed back, but then it was wrong again.

This may leave you more confused than before you started reading, as frequently there seems to be no way to get 100%. No matter what word you use, it can be wrong, while often using the wrong word will get you a higher percentage, and therefore a pass.

Computer programming language has a specific syntax and grammar, which is not the case for natural languages.

The passive voice, recognized as being more formal, is often marked down by machines and the active voice marked as the correct version.

This definitely promotes bad grammar and encourages extremely bad writing and therefore should be banned.

Linguists and English professors agree that grammar checkers are usually so inaccurate as to "do more harm than good" and "for the most part, accepting the advice of a computer grammar checker on your prose will make it much worse, sometimes hilariously incoherent".

Whoever invented these machines that "do the job of a human in one hundredth of the time, and just as well", cannot have known anything about grammar or writing.
First, English, which is the main language of the World Wide Web, comes in many and varied forms – all of which are considered correct by their respective countries.
As the inventors of these "time saving wonders" seem to be mostly American, it is that language that shows up as "correct", while anything else is often, if not usually, considered "wrong".

If one wanted to nit-pick, "English" is from England and is therefore what is commonly known as "The Queen's English", so anything else is wrong.

However, being human means being broad minded, so accepting the English used in America, Canada, Ireland, Australia, South Africa and all the other countries where English is the official language, comes as a given.

Writing is not always about using correct grammar, as there are occasions where "incorrect grammar" is actually correct. It conveys a meaning in a simple form; "He said as what he don't like it," instantly lets readers know this is an uncultured person, and may be a more elegant way to express this sentiment rather than using a simple 'he barely knows how to read and write', to describe the speaker.

If you speak to a person who says, "Me thinks he doeth protest too much", it is incorrect to write, when I spoke to him he said, "I believe he is protesting too much" yet this is what is needed to pass the mechanical grammar checker.

If you wish to say, "While on holiday in Italy, someone said, "*vuoi un gelato*?", and I assumed they were asking if I was cold, when they were actually enquiring if I wanted an ice-cream", will bring certain grammar failure, along with the advice; "run on sentences and incomplete phrase – you forgot the beginning".
Passive, well structures sentences are doubtful, as they also appear incorrect to some machines, so it is much better to write as if for a five-year-old imbecile, whose first language is not English. These are sure passes for grammar checkers, (Grammarly being the main culprit).

The machines also appear unable or un-programmed to distinguish between fact and fiction. There are many articles on the internet, passed by these mechanical checkers that say, "migraine is a headache". This is incorrect, not true and mis-leading. Migraine is a neurological disease, sometimes called a debilitating condition. What it is **not**, is a headache. However, one of the common symptoms of this condition is a headache, so a machine seeing the word "headache" associated with migraine believes this to be correct. It does not measure the positioning or use of the word.

Being "free" to write is now a thing of the past, if you let it be. You need to spend money buying programmes to ensure you comply with other programmes, making sure as much of your article as possible is "American" in structure.

Do not use these machines, use your own knowledge of the language, and yes, it is fine to run a story through a machine to check your work, but only accept corrections you are sure are right.

Grammar checkers are a sad lowering of standards for writing on the whole.

Free Resources for Writers, Dictionaries

Free Online Dictionaries

First, a good dictionary is useful, as it not only helps with vocabulary but also with specific theme related words, the origins of words and similar words. Some writers already have a dictionary installed and will have no need of another one, and there is one included in most word processing programmes - but these tend to be quite basic.

There are advantages to using an online dictionary;

- Price – if it is free
- It takes up no space on a computer and as it is online
- It is more current than a bought version, (most dictionaries do not have updates unless you buy the new version).

A good free dictionary to use online is; "The Free Dictionary", http://www.thefreedictionary.com/

The home page is very full of related and non-related items, but do not despair – it can be customised easily and quickly and your choices are memorised and remain for any subsequent visits.

This dictionary is used online, so you simple bookmark it or add it to your toolbar for ease of use.

When you look up a word, not only does the meaning appear but a few other options such as finding out more by clicking on a related link, (usually Wikipedia – not a reliable source), and translating the word into a host of other languages. The answers give multiple definitions and tell you what other dictionaries contain the word, (medical, legal etc. see below for a more comprehensive list). It tells you the origin of the word; you can listen to the pronunciation, (in both American and British English), synonyms, related words, antonyms and more.

The resources that are offered with this dictionary include:

- dictionary
- thesaurus
- medical dictionary
- legal dictionary
- financial dictionary
- idioms
- abbreviations
- encyclopaedia
- translation of a word
- many languages
- word games to help build vocabulary
- much more

This really is a useful little tool and although I have the Oxford English Dictionary installed on my computer, (I am British after all), I also use this online dictionary for technical terms, other languages and other features.

A great site to look for symptoms is The Thesaurus.com. It offers many synonyms, antonyms, examples and related words. This lets you easily vary your vocabulary.

https://www.thesaurus.com/

Checking for errors

Word does do quite a good job of catching errors, but it doesn't get them all, plus it shows certain things as mistakes, which are right.

Paperrater is a free place where you can check your work. The free version only lets you put about 3-4 pages at a time, so if you are working on a book, this can be time consuming, but it is the best I have found, and I tried many.

https://www.paperrater.com/

Free Plagiarism Checkers

Initially this may not be something you think you need, but it is a useful resource. So much has been written about so many things it is easy to write something in the same way as another person without intending to, but if you publish it, you could find yourself in trouble for copying or plagiarising work.

There are many programmes around to check if a piece of work is original, and many sites say they put your work through a certain programme to check this, so you may risk losing your good standing if your "original article" is found to be too similar to an existing piece.

I have tried many of these and found really none of them 100% accurate – even the most expensive and popular one.   I normally use four free ones and if they all give the same results I go with that and cross my fingers.

plagiarisma.net

The Free Plagiarism Checker on this site only allows a limited number of uses before asking you to join. Membership is free and they do not send spam or junk mail, so there is no reason not to join. I have been a member for some time and have not received one undesirable email.

Free membership entitles you to a limited number of searches per day, but these are enough for most writers' needs. You can upgrade for a small fee – or if you write about them and they approve the article or review, you get a free upgrade.

This programme can be used online or downloaded, (Windows).

Plagiarismnet goes one step further than other checkers and offers the alternative of checking for similarity and the results give the % of "sameness".

Another feature this software has that the others do not is that multiple languages are supported.

The results vary but give about 60% accuracy.

searchenginereports.net

This is low on my list as the results tend to be not as accurate as the others, but occasionally, by some stroke of luck, it does give information the others have missed.

When it does work, it is the best, but this only occurs around 60% of the time. It has given me "original content" for work I have already published, so if it says, "original", do not believe it and try another one, but if it says, "copied", believe it.

It tells you where the original work is, and even goes so far as to say that there are other copies predating this and where they too are. You can choose the level of "sameness", but the higher the level the slower the results are in coming, so be patient.

duplichecker.com

This too is a bit hit and miss, and like searchenginereports.net shows detail when found, but more often than not it does not find anything, even when you know it is there because you published it yourself! When a copy is found this programme shows where the copy is located.

This accepts text and files and while it says .txt documents only, I have used other extensions successfully.

This seems to be around 25 – 30% accurate.

dustball.com

This one seems fine, no more, no less. Once it has checked the document a "possible plagiarism" button appears, you click this and it shows you where the work in question is located. This is a Google page, but the relevant parts are highlighted for ease of use.

This is about 50% accurate.

With all these programmes, "no copies found" is not necessarily true but "plagiarism detected" is.

Free, Legal Images

You need a cover for your book if you are going to self-publish, and even some publishers want a finished product, so require this too.

Royalty Free Images are usually not free. This is just a marketing strategy to hook you in and these companies want money which they call by another name, but as Shakespeare might have said, "A Royalty by any other name..".

Before using an image that is not your own, from anywhere on the internet, read the terms carefully and follow any "rights" related guidelines. For truly free images this is usually attribution and occasionally a link to the creator. Each site will tell you what is required.

This is a list of sites that offer free, legal images a writer, or anyone for that matter, can use.

Pexels have top quality photos, some totally free, others which ask for attribution. I tend to give attribution even if not asked for, after all someone has created this work and they deserve recognition. There is a massive range of excellent quality photos of all sorts of subject matter.

https://www.pexels.com

Wikimedia Commons has a huge range of photographs, symbols and designs and appears to be attribution only. The range is vast, nearly too much so, and the possibilities of refining a search are just about nil. This means trolling through a large number of poor quality images to find a good one that suits your purpose. If you persevere there is a good chance you will find what you were looking for, but for some reason many or even most of the images are not nearly as good quality as other sites. Sometimes the image is poor it may have an ugly background or extra items not related to the one thing you want to show.

I use this for historic photos or obscure places, in short, things that are hard to find anywhere else.

http://commons.wikimedia.org/wiki/Main_Page

Flickr is crowd sourced and that means you never know what you will find. People take pictures of the strangest things and even post totally out of focus images, but again the choice is huge and well worth a visit if you cannot find the image elsewhere. This is also attribution and often a link back to the owner required.

http://www.flickr.com/

Morgue File and Stock Exchange are good sites and are quite similar in many ways. The pictures on Morgue Files have a better look to them, and don't ask me what I mean as it is just a feeling of being better photos, but both sites give a good range and you can search by keywords, categories etc. on Morgue files, but not on Stock Exchange.
Some photographs on Stock Exchange are not free, so you do need to look carefully at the ones you have chosen to use. These generally come up as "premium results" and are in a band at the top, and when you enlarge there are prices.

Otherwise both sites work on "image credit", so use away.

The best place of all for images is Every Stock Photo, but things are not quite as they seem. This is a site that looks through other sites, (about 12 including the ones mentioned above), for exactly the image you want – and the results are amazing.
There are two main problems as I see it. One, the results are around 80% from Flickr, and users on that site tend to give titles that make sense only to themselves. Stonehenge has a title "A Horseshoe", for example, so if you are looking for Stonehenge that picture will not show up, and if you were looking for a horseshoe, well, you get Stonehenge.
The other problem is each site has its own image rights terms and conditions, so you need to read them all before deciding which image suits or in deed using it.
The site does let you filter results by licence, source, (you can remove Flickr), size etc, so you can choose which sites are searched.

The interesting thing about these resources is that many are actually better than their expensive counterparts. I can only assume they are free because some brand names have conquered the market and there is little room for other, paying programmes. This is a shame when so many are really good.

N.B. beware of Google images. Many of their pictures are there without the owners permission. I had a photo I put on trip advisor which Google had put on Google Images without my permission and I had to send another DMCA Takedown notice to get it removed.

Language Translators

A mechanical language translator can be useful device if used for fun, a hobby or private reasons, but not as a work tool.

You may find information in another language and want to know what it says to include, or not, in a piece you are writing, but many of these translators are far from accurate. If they spew out total garbage you can see it does not make sense but if they give you a reasonable looking bit of information, you may believe it to be true. In many cases it is not what the original said.

There are two translators that are accurate enough for most private uses, and I have tried many machines. I have only used simple French and Spanish and Italian and cannot vouch for any other languages, (even my French is a bit limited), but they work well enough to give an idea of the article.

Frengly and Lookwayup

Both support many languages and give reasonable translations much of the time. They do, however work on small pieces of text, so a short paragraph is about all you can do at one time.

I am a translator by profession, and am now just about unemployable as companies do not see any reason to pay me lots of dollars when a machine will do it free.

"Our company confirms once again to be always in the forefront, showing the new range of products certified by the Rina. We undertook the whole course of the Italian nautical field from 1926 living the lead role during the different stages of a marketing in constantly development. We was the first company to homologate in the 1995."

One company who turned down my bid to translate from Italian to English for them published this.

It should have said; "Our company is in the forefront in its field of cosmetics. All out products are carefully tested and certified before going to market. We have been shipping abroad with enormous success since 1926. We were the first cosmetics company to go green in 1995

Of course that too is a lot of rubbish, and not true, but at least it is understandable..

As these people do not speak English, they believe this to be accurate and clear, but more importantly, it is free. The fact it will not bring in new business is not considered.

That said, if you want to include a phrase in a foreign language, or fact check something not in English, try two sites to be sure of accuracy.

http://frengly.com/#

http://lookwayup.com/free/trans.htm

Chapter 4 Where to Earn Money Writing Until your Book Takes Off

Here are a few sites you can earn money writing while waiting for your big break.

Every writing site I have tried, (and I think I have tried them all), is more or less the same, and they are far from perfect.

They all say they take a percentage, usually around 20%, but you will find strange 'taxes' and other expenses also come out of your share, making your earnings 75%, not 80%.

The sites also seem to ignore the fact that without the writers they would have no work. Their money comes mainly from clients, so they bend over backwards to keep them happy, while throwing writers under the bus to do so. Once you have earned your money it can take up to three weeks before you get it – longer than they appear to tell you.

None of them is set up well, and none work well, even though it is not hard to make a few changes to get things running smoother, better and therefore bring them a much better return.

The first problem is competition from non-writers who 'blow their own trumpet louder than yours', and will do it for pennies.

I have seen jobs advertised 'Book wanted – 30-35,000 words, payment $20, and it had 53 offers to do it!

Another job was for 500,000 words delivered in three weeks and one person bid $20 to deliver the work in three days.

You cannot compete with that, so don't try. If the client wants to pay $20, or wants a huge tome written quicker than physically possible, they are not interested in quality, they want quick and cheap.

This is a genuine profile description by a writer who has 98% feedback over 87 jobs, (believe it or not). The site rates them in the top bracket of their workers. Something is seriously wrong when a site is prepared to list this person as 'one of our top members'.

I am XXXXX, a fulltime, a quick a efficient writer, perfect for your writing me based project.
Now I want to explore the era of my interest, I writing.
Writing, is an inherent quality of mine and I want to flourish in this fields.
I am swift in typing and have a very good command on English. My pieces in content are unique, errors-free, plagiarisms-free and well-researched. I take my time to deliver   quickly   and   perfect.
My motto is to satisfy client with best quality and skill in me   through   my   writings.
I have a widespread vocabulary range and am excellent

When I worked as an English teacher I would have marked this as 10%, and that only because they did their homework. Where to start correcting this… basically it isn't something I would correct, as it all needs re-done.

The other problem is you need good feedback to get work, but you can't get work until you have feedback. The answer to this is; find a low paying, but simple job; '300 word blog for $8'. If it says what the blog is about, write it as part of your proposal and offer it for $5. If you get a few of these, with good feedback, you are ready to start seriously.

Each site has jobs posted and you send your proposal. They chose a writer, deposit the money into escrow, you do the job, it is approved and the money is released.

Here are 4 sites I use and where I make money, although not always huge amounts.

People Per Hour (PPH)
(https://www.peopleperhour.com/freelance-jobs/writing)

Count on 25% going to the site in one way or another. Once clients have paid, they release the money immediately and when you request payment it happened quickly, within 1-2 days generally. That recently changed to be 21 days, (due to Covid they said, but I fail to understand why Covid can cause them to take 21 days to press a button to release funds.)

If there are any problems, such as clients disappearing, (which happens more often that you may imagine), they release the funds in escrow after 7 days.

If a client complains they do not want to pay as they feel the work is not up to standard, PPH tend to take the client's side. I had a client, for 10 articles, do this, (and I found she had published all 10 on her website), and PPH allowed her not to pay. I complained, pointing out she had used my work illegally, without payment, and after 3 months, and many, many emails, they agreed I was right. In the meantime I sent a DMCA takedown notice to her site hosts. (Stolen or plagiarised content is removed from a website at the request of the owner of the copyright. The site might also be closed.) Her web site was closed down almost immediately. I had to pay £9 to send a formal complaint to PPH, which I got back because I won – but this is ridiculous and one of the many examples where the client is preferred over the worker.

The highest paying jobs tend to be on this site, but mainly for articles/blogs and so on, not books.

There are some very high paying jobs, and some low paying but very quick ones, (write 2 quiz questions for $15).

You get a certain amount of 'proposals' free each month and can buy more. I never pay for more, and select carefully what I bid on.

The standard of client and work here, I find to be much higher than other sites. They also cater to many other fields, designs, photographers, accountants etc

Upwork (https://www.upwork.com)

Again fees etc. eat up around 25% of whatever you are paid. Money sits in 'pending' for up to a week. Then it can take another 4-5 days, or more, before you get it. I generally count 3 weeks before I can have access to my earnings.

There are more jobs on here than other sites, but clients tend to be too vague 'need writer for 4 blogs per week,' but they fail to say what subject. On PPH you can ask 'clarification questions', but on Upwork you have to pay to do that.

You also get a certain number of bids, or 'connects' as they call them, every month.

Clients leave feedback twice, one is public and one is secret.

My first four jobs all had public feedback of 5 star, therefore 100%. Each client asked me for more work, so they must have liked it. However once my secret feedback was published, (yes, it isn't as secret as it should be, it is merely anonymous), I went down to 72%.

One of my clients had left me 1 star feedback on every aspect, (there are a few topics; delivery time; accuracy, skill etc.) I contacted the site, pointing out one set of feedback was obviously a lie, but was told it was their 'opinion', and they had a right to that. They refused to accept that a client who really thought my work was that bad would not have asked for more. They refused to acknowledge that 'secret' feedback should not show up on my profile, or that by asking for two different kinds of vote, they were encouraging people to lie. The bad marks remained and I found it difficult to get work to boost my rating. (I managed it eventually.)

There are quite a few jobs ghost writing books, both fiction and non on this site, as well as articles. Unfortunately pay is often low.

Freelancer (https://www.freelancer.com)

Many jobs are low paying, some very low, and there are many bids for these. That said, you get free bids each month and so trying costs nothing. I have had people accept my bid, which was the highest by far, as they thought my work worth it.

I struggle to get work here, mainly because the jobs tend to offer so little payment, I don't bother to bid. That said, the site takes 10%, considerably less that the others.

There are plenty of article writing gigs here, but few books.

Payment is around a week (small charge to send money, generally $0.99)

Guru (https://www.guru.com)

Like the other sites you get monthly free bids, so trying costs nothing.

Payment is very low, but the length required is often short. If you are quick, you could fit in a 10,000 word book while looking for better paying work.

There are other writing sites as well, but having tried them, I found them a waste of time. That doesn't mean they won't work for you, so look around and see what there is. be wary of ones who offer payment per click for your work, this seldom pays more than a few pence, and you need to promote your work to get even that. Promoting it takes you away from writing time so is counter-productive.

Chapter 5 How to decide if Self-Publishing is really for you

You have written a book and want to see it in print, but there are too many options and you do not know where to start. The next step is to evaluate the advantages of normal publishing, self-publishing, subsidiary publishing, print-on-demand or ebook publishing.

This article evaluates the pros and cons of self-publishing.

- Pros
  - You are the publisher and as such have total say in how your book is produced. What graphics are used, how it is set out, what the jacket and title are and everything else.
  - There are no editors, publishers and agents all taking a cut of your earnings.
  - No one can tell you to remove a piece that may well be your favorite part of the story.
  - You choose the price for the book and any sales or discounts.
  - All rights to the book remain in your hands.
  - You can publish material that publishing houses do not want to touch. This could be a book on a specialized subject or poetry, as these are not best sellers and do not generate enough income for many publishing houses to be interested.

- The book will appear on the market much sooner than if published through a publishing company.
- If you have a ready-made reading public, (for instance, someone who is expert in one field and gives talks, can sell the book at these talks), this allows more freedom to write and more profit when sold.

- Cons
  - You have to pay to buy copies of your print book, unless you only make an eBook, to give away.
  - Although all the profits are yours alone, so are any costs, (perhaps paying an artist to make the cover), so this can make it difficult to make any profit.
  - You need to market the book yourself otherwise no one will know it exists, what it is about or where to buy it.
  - If you simply want the joy of having your writing in book form, look at other options like print-on-demand, as a few copies will do. Vanity publishing, as this is called, only really makes sales to friends and family who feel they have to buy your work.
  - Not only is a large amount of cash needed, to self publish, but also a lot of time to edit, format and so on, so you will not have time to write a sequel or second book.
  - Self-published books are regarded as "not published" by the literary world. You will find it

difficult if not impossible to find someone willing to review your book, shops will be reluctant to stock it and libraries do not want one book when they can have multiple titles from a big publisher.

- You need to edit and proof read carefully, and this is usually easier on work that is not your own, simply because you already know what you wanted to say and understand your phrase, while others may find it incomplete or difficult to follow.
- You need to obtain book ISBN code to have any chance of success, and these can cost.
- You need to format the book and source designs and graphics.
- Storing the books once they are printed and shipped is your responsibility, and this may take more space than you think, and some self-publishers oblige you to take a set number.
- Marketing has to be done by you.
- Advertising is also up to you.
- Even if you manage to generate sales, you need to take orders and deliver the books.
- You may need a business license to self-publish, so find out from the authorities in your country.

All in all the cons outweigh the pros, so you need to be sure this is the right choice for your work and you need quite large funds, time and resources. Self-publishing has worked very well for a few people, but they are in the minority.

Chapter 6 Getting a Novel Published

Getting a novel published is more difficult than finding gold. Many publishers do not accept unsolicited manuscripts, so this means you need to be known to them before they will even read your work.

Small independent publishers are often the easiest way to start as they have less rigid procedures. Search for any that publish the genre you have written. A literary agency is another possibility as they will get in touch with publishers for you, but they want a percentage of any money you earn and often this contract will last for multiple books if you are successful. Read it carefully and do not accept any terms you are worried about. Ask if they can be changed/removed. Sometimes this does happen.

Once you find suitable publishers, read the authors guidelines for each publisher, as if you send material they do not want, your query may be automatically discarded. At this stage some want only a synopsis, while others want the first pages and some require the full book.

Write an introductory cover letter that is short and concise. This includes who you are, any experience, (be honest they may check and if they discover any discrepancies may well black list you), and summarize the book. This should be only two or three paragraphs long as all publishers receive innumerable new books every day and often feel disinclined to read long winded letters.

Send this to any suitable publishers and wait for four to eight weeks. Some publishers give time frames for their answer, so wait the appropriate time, and then send another email asking if they have received your work and when you can expect to hear something.

If your work is rejected do not give up. Some companies tell you why they are not interested and you should reread your manuscript, looking at what they say and see if any adjustments will help. If no reason was given just keep sending your work to other publishers until you either have enough rejections to let you know the work is not good enough, or an acceptance.

I had a story rejected many times before selling it to a client. It was published on Amazon, under the client's name, and went into the top 5 in its category.

If your book is accepted you will probably need to get a lawyer's advice on the contract, to be sure you are not signing something that is only in favor of the publisher and has no advantages to you.

Remember that an advance is just that, and is deducted from your earnings at a later stage. The size of the advance may indicate how many copies a publisher thinks will sell – they will not offer you $5,000 if they believe sales will total $100, but an advance of $10 does not necessarily mean they believe sales will be low. The only advantage of a large advance is if you need money urgently, and it does make the published keener to push sales as they need to recoup this money.

Chapter 7 Tips and Challenges to Improve your Writing

I am an English teacher and published author.

I will set you challenges to help you improve your writing, (hopefully). Each of rhe challenges 1,2,4, 5 and 6 are designed to help with one particular aspect of writing; plot/story, descriptions, timeline, characters, style/tone.

This is not a lesson it is simple a few exercises intended to help your writing.

1. Write a 500 word story. Now write it again in 150/100 words only. Are the 300-400 words you took out necessary? Do they add anything to the story? If not, leave them out.
2. Choose an area/place, write an under 500 word description and make the reader see the room/beach/clearing etc
3. Create an obstacle in your story and get round it
4. Write under 1,000 words about 2 main characters. Make readers love/sympathise with one and hate/fear one. Not a list of qualities, an explanation about/of them. This can be divided into sections in a book with one person describing a character in one part and another doing it later on, or it can all be together.
5. Write an under 1,000 word story and draw it on a timeline graph. Start the line from the first date in your story and draw, without lifting off the paper

until the story ends. Is the line a mess and hard to follow or is it tidy and easy to see? It doesn't need to be straight, just easy to follow, even if there are many turns)

6. Write an under 500 word story written from a Zebra's point of view. He can talk to other animals or humans.

This is not as stupid as it seems. When writing it can be important to learn to write from another person's perspective and in a different voice. A zebra is only an exaggeration of that.

7. Write an opening paragraph that makes readers want to read more.

8. Write a closing paragraph that leaves readers wanting to see another of your stories.

9. Write a brief outline showing what the story needs for it to work well, character – who, why; plot that is credible etc

10. Write a dialogue between people that lasts at least 20 expressions, (not from the same person.

11. Re-write these sentences removing the repeated words and replacing them with different expressions while keeping the meaning the same.

12. Create atmosphere Eg; I was in my garden and I heard him speaking from behind the dividing wall.
OR
There was a tall wooden wall between my garden and his, and as I stood there I suddenly heard a voice saying something. It came from behind the

wall. Not being able to see him made it sound eerie.

13. Do not overdue the final checking/changing. It is easy to take good work and work on it too much so it flows less that it did. Stop as soon as you feel it is good. Come back a few days later and check again.

14. Do check your facts. If you write it got dark in New York at five in the afternoon, check that really is when darkness falls. I read a book by a top selling author who said 'Buon nuit' instead of 'bonne nuit', and even then they did not mean goodnight, they meant 'good evening'.

15. Don't mistake mystery with obscurity

    Don't get caught in the trap of thinking that just because something is difficult to understand, it will create an air of mystery that will draw the reader in. This is rarely true. Don't sacrifice clarity for cleverness. People generally don't enjoy reading things that are obscure, whether this effect was achieved on purpose or accidentally. Resist the urge to be complicated for the sake of being complicated.

Tips

I write down my protagonist's names, jobs etc. and keep it at the end of the story as I write. That was I can see quickly 'David is married to Jennifer. He is an accountant.'

After a few books, characters tend to run together a bit; this just makes it easy to check who a person is.

I never check my writing until I have finished. It interrupts the flow, but that is only me. I know other writers who check as they go along, so find what works best for you.

Writing & Ghost Writing: tips, hints and stories

Get clear instructions up front and ask as many questions as needed before you start – eg. Are there any names you want? Any you don't want?

Many want 25 pages which they say is 10,000 words – generally it isn't. It is 7,000 – 8,000. Ask which they want. If it is 25 pages, you save 2,000 words, therefore earn more.

Don't be afraid to point out obvious things. I had a client who wanted John, James, Johnny and Jack. I said I thought readers would struggle to remember which was which because the names were too similar, so we went with Philip, James, Michael and Will.

Point out that someone who says they will write 500,000 words for $20 in 3 days, is probably lying, (unless they have it already written), and the chances they are rubbish for that price, are very, very high – and yes that exact offer was made.

If it is romance, ask which sub-genre? And do they want it 'steamy'?

Unfortunately, although I have no idea who my clients are, I can say some of them are idiots who know nothing about books. I had a client who wanted a Regency Romance. I love these, so was happy, but the price was low for any book, especially this one. I pointed out that there was so much checking of terms, such as 'vouchers for Almacks' – I wasn't sure of the spelling – necktie terms etc to do, I would like paid more than she was offering. She had no idea what I meant and said 'I only needed to put the date to make it regency; just write a modern romance and say it is 1840 at the beginning'.

Most clients have no idea what a first draft is and I get comments like; 'secrret' is spelt wrong on page 15; it isn't Monday; John is not David's brother; comitment is spelt wrong…

I always tell them up front – I will send a first draft which will have mistakes, but I will correct these at the end. Yet still they point out a host of errors.

Make sure your client is happy. It is worth the extra work to make this happen as negative feedback takes forever to build back up.

Get money into escrow before you start. Never do work without the money being present. I ended up with 177 articles I had no use for because clients did not pay, (they had not seen the work, so it wasn't a question of quality, they just vanished. And yes, being trusting by nature, it did take me that long to figure it out.)

Be careful of contracts – many say you did not copy and are responsible if it is found you did, (fair enough), but they also tend to say the client can change it in any fashion they want – also fair enough. The problem arises if or when the contract says, 'you did not copy and are responsible once it is published if it is found you did'. Once you hand it over, the client can put in anything they wish, and maybe they plagiarised something. Get them to change that to read 'you did not copy and are responsible **for the work you delivered**, if it is found you did. Keep a copy. (I have a USB with all the books I wrote on it.

Always put a longer delivery date than necessary. You never know when a problem will arise. A broken tooth can set you back a day, and if your deadline is tight this might make you late. That means the client can refuse to pay, or offer to pay half, or less. Again, it can mean negative feedback.

Remember costs; the site, many of which charge 20%, which actually ends up being 25% as they add taxes, or so they say. Then bank or money transfers can cost, and it can also cost you to receive money, (like on PayPal). The $100 you thought you would get quickly becomes $70.

Writer's Rant

After dealing with a string of stupid clients and their impossible requests, I sat down and wrote a letter to the latest one. It was never destined for him, it was simply a way for me to say what I really wanted to say instead of what I did say. The contents of this are exact, but I was polite and understanding. I put it more delicately.

I wrote it as we were communicating. It wasn't a hard or long job, and the pay was reasonable – the problem was the client wasn't.

Letter

OK, so you give all these stupid instructions and expect me to follow them. How the devil do you think that is possible? Did your brain get swept away with the last hurricane?

'I want it done quickly, sometime within the next 30 minutes if possible, but take the time to make sure it is right'.

Have you heard yourself? Do you not realise this makes no sense? I suppose not, otherwise you wouldn't have said it.

By, 'the time to make sure it is right', do you mean the 1 minute that remains after I have hurriedly written 800 words in 29 minutes?

I know Marie Antoinette said it was possible to have your cake and eat it, but remember they did cut off her head, so she couldn't eat the cake, even if there was any left.

Time to make up your mind buddy – do you want it quick or good? Oops, I just realised, to make up your mind, you need a thought process, and that requires a brain. Forget I just said that.

Toss a coin, not in the bin but up in the air; heads I do it quickly, tails I do it well.

What I really said was, "I m afraid I cannot do both. I can do it as quickly as possible and then take the time to check it is good, or I can just send it without checking. Not both. I am afraid I need you to choose which.

On the subject of me doing two pieces of work for you; I have heard people say silly things but I have never seen anyone courageous enough to write them down. I asked you for a total of £100 and you replied, 'I will pay you per article, £25 + £25 = £100'. I hate to be the one to have to tell you, but this is not right. It should be £75 + £75 = £100, (I do so hope you believe this), so after the first article you need to give me £75 and after the second one another £75.

This is more or less exact, just slightly more cutting here.

Now about the topics, are you sure you want an article on the *conservatory* government in Britain? Well, you replied quickly, and you are sure, somehow I thought you might be. Maybe you mean the Conservative Government?

When you say conservatory government, do you mean Conservative Government?

There is no need to insult me. I am well aware they are also called 'Tory', but it isn't because they are a conservatory. I will not explain it to you as there is no chance you will ever understand. This, however, just might be something you can comprehend – a conservatory is a glass room attached to a house, not a political party. I probably should not have used the word 'party' as you are now imagining a room full of people with drink and music.

I do know they are also called Tories, but their real name is Conservative Government, not conservatory government. There is no such thing.

What? You wonder if I am the right person to do this job and the other on a Labrador Government.

I'm not. When you find someone prepared to write about the British Labrador Government, never mind the Conservatory Government, you will have found the perfect writer for you. I am sure you will get someone as there are some really dumb people out there, and you should know.

I just left out the part about dumb people.

Why do you get so insulted when someone calls you an idiot? It isn't as if you understand the meaning of the word.

I will not do this job, so you can save enough money to get a new battery for your brain because this one is definitely not working.

Many clients have unreasonable requests, so read their instructions carefully and do not commit to anything you are not sure you can do.

Conclusion

It is not impossible to be successful, but it is hard, much more so now that it was some years ago. Many people from non-English speaking countries believe they can write well in English. Probably some of them can, but they are in the minority. The problem is the ones who say they can, charge very much less than you would work for, and they are your competition.

Take as an example 50 Shades of Grey. This has to be one of the worst written books in the history of publishing. That is not only my opinion, but many reviews say the same thing;

"It is written in the style you'd expect from an illiterate teenager."

"I bought this book, mainly out of curiosity, but also to see if it was as appallingly-written as people say. It's much, much worse than that."

"If any part of this book had been written as an O-level English composition it would have failed dismally"

"The writing is poor; it does not flow and a sentence longer than five or six words is hard to find. *"For me, this is smart." "I inwardly sigh." "I flush." "I hope."* (There is a lot of sighing and lip biting.) This is so stilted it is hard to get beyond the first page, never mind finish the whole punishment. The vocabulary is very limited with the same banal words repeated over and over and over again. It is as if having finally found a word to describe something the writer thought it good to use that word as much as possible. (Some expressions are used nearly a hundred times in this piece of infantile drivel.) It is an insult to writers everywhere to call this a book. It is like a childish fantasy diary written by a five-year-old sick child."

Yet, this was a best seller and everyone loved it, while I couldn't dislike it or find it any more pathetic.

That goes to show, I know nothing, as I felt it was only fit to use as kindling for the fire.

For this reason, take me advice and think about whether it is useful or not and act accordingly. Do not consider what I say to be the absolute truth, I don't think anyone knows that. It is simply intended to help you along your path to writing.

NOTE: Remember copying another's work is a crime – everyone knows that, right? Well, it appears not. Many jobs are offered where they want you to model a book on another.

Modelling a book on another is both unethical and illegal.

The 'Fair Use' Rule: When Use of Copyrighted Material Is Unacceptable

Five Considerations Regarding "Fair Use"

Rule 2: Are Your Competing With the Source You're Copying From?

Without consent, you cannot use another person's protected expression in a way that impairs (or even potentially impairs) the market for his or her work.

Rule 5: The Quality of the Material Used Is as Important as the Quantity

The more important the material is to the original work, the less likely your use of it will be considered fair.

In one case a court ruled that something was not a fair use because the material quoted was the "heart of the book... the most interesting and moving parts of the entire manuscript,"

So, if you take the story idea used in a book, and write another, but different story around that, you are committing a crime on two levels.